The FIRST 100 CHINESE CHARACTERS

The quick and easy way to learn the basic Chinese characters

SIMPLIFIED CHARACTER EDITION

Introduction by
Alison and Laurence Matthews

TUTTLE Publishing

Tokyo | Rutland, Vermont | Singapore

THE TUTTLE STORY
"Books to Span the East and West"

Our core mission at Tuttle Publishing is to create books which bring people together one page at a time. Tuttle was founded in 1832 in the small New England town of Rutland, Vermont (USA). Our fundamental values remain as strong today as they were then—to publish best-in-class books informing the English-speaking world about the countries and peoples of Asia. The world has become a smaller place today and Asia's economic, cultural and political influence has expanded, yet the need for meaningful dialogue and information about this diverse region has never been greater. Since 1948, Tuttle has been a leader in publishing books on the cultures, arts, cuisines, languages and literatures of Asia. Our authors and photographers have won numerous awards and Tuttle has published thousands of books on subjects ranging from martial arts to paper crafts. We welcome you to explore the wealth of information available on Asia at **www.tuttlepublishing.com**.

Published by Tuttle Publishing, an imprint of Periplus Editions (HK) Ltd.

www.tuttlepublishing.com

LCC Card No. 2009387018
ISBN 978-0-8048-4992-0
(Published previously under 978-0-8048-3830-6)

Distributed by:

North America, Latin America & Europe
Tuttle Publishing, 364 Innovation Drive
North Clarendon, VT 05759-9436
Tel: 1 (802) 773 8930; Fax: 1 (802) 773 6993
info@tuttlepublishing.com
www.tuttlepublishing.com

Japan
Tuttle Publishing, Yaekari Building 3F 5-4-12 Osaki,
Shinagawa-ku Tokyo 141-0032, Japan
Tel: (81) 3 5437 0171; Fax: (81) 3 5437 0755
sales@tuttle.co.jp
www.tuttle.co.jp

Asia-Pacific
Berkeley Books Pte Ltd, 3 Kallang Sector #04-01/02
Singapore 349278
Tel: (65) 6741-2178; Fax: (65) 6741-2179
inquiries@periplus.com.sg
www.tuttlepublishing.com

23 22 21 20   10 9 8 7 6 5   2005VP
Printed in Malaysia

Contents

Introduction

Learning the characters is one of the most fascinating and fun parts of learning Chinese, and people are often surprised by how much they enjoy being able to recognize them and to write them. Added to that, *writing* the characters is also the best way of *learning* them. This book shows you how to write the second 100 most common characters and gives you plenty of space to practice writing them. When you do this, you'll be learning a writing system which is one of the oldest in the world and is now used by more than a billion people around the globe every day.

In this introduction we'll talk about:
- how the characters developed;
- the difference between traditional and simplified forms of the characters;
- what the "radicals" are and why they're useful;
- how to count the writing strokes used to form each character;
- how to look up the characters in a dictionary;
- how words are created by joining two characters together; and, most importantly;
- how to write the characters!

Also, in case you're using this book on your own without a teacher, we'll tell you how to get the most out of using it.

Chinese characters are not nearly as strange and complicated as people seem to think. They're actually no more mysterious than musical notation, which most people can master in only a few months. So there's really nothing to be scared of or worried about: everyone can learn them—it just requires a bit of patience and perseverance. There are also some things which you may have heard about writing Chinese characters that aren't true. In particular, you don't need to use a special brush to write them (a ball-point pen is fine), and you don't need to be good at drawing (in fact you don't even need to have neat handwriting, although it helps!).

How many characters are there?
Thousands! You would probably need to know something like two thousand to be able to read Chinese newspapers and books, but you don't need anything like that number to read a menu, go shopping or read simple street signs and instructions. Just as you can get by in most countries knowing about a hundred words of the local language, so too you can get by in China quite well knowing a hundred

common Chinese characters. And this would also be an excellent basis for learning to read and write Chinese.

How did the characters originally develop?
Chinese characters started out as pictures representing simple objects, and the first characters originally resembled the things they represented. For example:

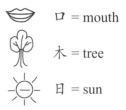

口 = mouth

木 = tree

日 = sun

Some other simple characters were pictures of "ideas":

一 one   二 two   三 three

Some of these characters kept this "pictographic" or "ideographic" quality about them, but others were gradually modified or abbreviated until many of them now look nothing like the original objects or ideas.

Then, as words were needed for things which weren't easy to draw, existing characters were "combined" to create new characters. For example, 女 (meaning "woman") combined with 子 (meaning "child") gives a new character 好 (which means "good" or "to be fond of").

Notice that when two characters are joined together like this to form a new character, they get squashed together and deformed slightly. This is so that the new, combined character will fit into the same size square or "box" as each of the original two characters. For example the character 日 "sun" becomes thinner when it is the left-hand part of the character 时 "time"; and it becomes shorter when it is the upper part of the character 星 "star". Some components got distorted and deformed even more than this in the combining process: for example when the character 人 "man" appears on the left-hand side of a complex character it gets compressed into 亻, like in the character 他 "he".

So you can see that some of the simpler characters often act as basic "building blocks" from which more complex characters are formed. This means that if you learn how to write these simple characters you'll also be learning how to write some complex ones too.

How are characters read and pronounced?

The pronunciations in this workbook refer to modern standard Chinese. This is the official language of China and is also known as "Mandarin" or "**putonghua**".

The pronunciation of Chinese characters is written out with letters of the alphabet using a romanization system called "Hanyu Pinyin"—or "**pinyin**" for short. This is the modern system used in China. In pinyin some of the letters have a different sound than in English—but if you are learning Chinese you'll already know this. We could give a description here of how to pronounce each sound, but it would take up a lot of space—and this workbook is about writing the characters, not pronouncing them! In any case, you really need to hear a teacher (or recording) pronounce the sounds out loud to get an accurate idea of what they sound like.

Each Chinese character is pronounced using only one syllable. However, in addition to the syllable, each character also has a particular *tone*, which refers to how the pitch of the voice is used. In standard Chinese there are four different tones, and in pinyin the tone is marked by placing an accent mark over the vowel as follows:

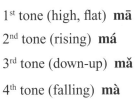
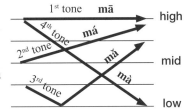

1st tone (high, flat) **mā**

2nd tone (rising) **má**

3rd tone (down-up) **mǎ**

4th tone (falling) **mà**

The pronunciation of each character is therefore a combination of a syllable and a tone. There are only a small number of available syllables in Chinese, and many characters therefore share the same syllable—in fact many characters share the same sound plus tone combination. They are like the English words "here" and "hear"—when they are spoken, you can only tell which is which from the context or by seeing the word in written form.

Apart from **putonghua** (modern standard Chinese), another well-known type of Chinese is Cantonese, which is spoken in southern China and in many Chinese communities around the world. In fact there are several dozen different Chinese languages, and the pronunciations of Chinese characters in these languages are all very different from each other. But the important thing to realize is that the characters themselves do *not* change. So two Chinese people who can't understand each other when they're talking together, can write to one another without any problem at all!

Simplified and traditional characters

As more and more characters were introduced over the years by combining existing characters, some of them became quite complicated. Writing them required many strokes which was time-consuming, and it became difficult to distinguish some of them, especially when the writing was small. So when writing the characters quickly in hand-written form, many people developed short-cuts and wrote them in a more simplified form. In the middle of the 20th century, the Chinese decided to create a standardised set of simplified characters to be used by everyone in China. This resulted in many of the more complicated characters being given simplified forms, making them much easier to learn and to write. Today in China, and also in Singapore, these simplified characters are used almost exclusively, and many Chinese no longer learn the old traditional forms. However the full traditional forms continue to be used in Taiwan and in overseas Chinese communities around the world.

Here are some examples of how some characters were simplified:

Traditional		Simplified
見	→	见
飯	→	饭
號	→	号
幾	→	几

Modern standard Chinese uses only simplified characters. But it is useful to be able to recognize the traditional forms as they are still used in many places outside China, and of course older books and inscriptions were also written using the traditional forms. This workbook teaches the full simplified forms. If there is a traditional form, then it is shown in a separate box on the right-hand side of the page so that you can see what it looks like. Where there is no traditional form, the character was considered simple enough already and was left unchanged.

How is Chinese written?

Chinese was traditionally written from top to bottom in columns beginning on the right-hand side of the page and working towards the left, like this:

幸福一点儿也不
难拥有。只要你
常为人着想，带
来欢乐，你会发
觉到那也是一种
幸福呀！

This means that for a book printed in this way, you start by opening it at (what Westerners would think of as) the back cover. While writing in columns is sometimes considered archaic, you will still find many books, especially novels and more serious works of history, printed in this way.

Nowadays, though, most Chinese people write from left to right in horizontal lines working from the top of a page to the bottom, just as we do in English.

Are Chinese characters the same as English words?
Although each character has a meaning, it's not really true that an individual character is equivalent to an English "word". Each character is actually only a single *syllable*. In Chinese (like in English) some words are just one syllable, but most words are made up of two or more syllables joined together. The vast majority of words in Chinese actually consist of two separate characters placed together in a pair. These multi-syllable words are often referred to as "compounds", and this workbook provides a list of common compounds for each character.

Some Chinese characters are one-syllable words on their own (like the English words "if" and "you"), while other characters are only ever used as one half of a word (like the English syllables "sen" and "tence"). Some characters do both: they're like the English "light" which is happy as a word on its own, but which also links up to form words like "headlight" or "lighthouse".

The Chinese write sentences by stringing characters together in a long line from left to right (or in a column from top to bottom), with equal-sized spaces between each character. If English were written this way—as individual syllables rather than as words that are joined together—it would mean all the syllables would be written separately with spaces in between them, something like this:

If you can un der stand this sen tence you can read Chi nese too.

So in theory, you can't see which characters are paired together to form words, but in practice, once you know a bit of Chinese, you can!

Punctuation was not traditionally used when writing Chinese, but today commas, periods (full stops), quotation marks, and exclamation points are all used along with other types of punctuation which have been borrowed from English.

Two ways of putting characters together
We have looked at *combining characters* together to make new *characters*, and *pairing characters* together to make *words*. So what's the difference?

Well, when two *simple characters* are combined to form a new *complex character*, they are squashed or distorted so that the new character fits into the same size square as the original characters. The meaning of the new character *may* be related to the meaning of its components, but it frequently appears to have no connection with them at all! The new complex character also has a new single-syllable pronunciation, which may or may not be related to the pronunciation of one of its parts. For example:

女		也		她
nǔ	+	**yě**	=	**tā**
woman		also		she

日		月		明
rì	+	**yuè**	=	**míng**
sun		moon/month		bright

On the other hand, when characters are *paired together* to create *words*, the characters are simply written one after the other, normal sized, with a normal space in between (and there are no hyphens or anything to show that these characters are working together as a pair). The resulting word has a pronunciation which is *two* syllables—it is simply the pronunciations of the two individual characters one after the other. Also, you're much more likely to be able to guess the meaning of the word from the meanings of the individual characters that make it up. For example:

大		人		大人
dà	+	**rén**	=	**dà rén**
big		person		adult

姐		妹		姐妹
jiě	+	**mèi**	=	**jiě mèi**
older sister		younger sister		sisters

四		月		四月
sì	+	**yuè**	=	**sì yuè**
four		moon/month		April

再		见		再见
zài	+	**jiàn**	=	**zài jiàn**
again		see; meet		Goodbye!

Is it necessary to learn words as well as characters?
As we've said, the meaning of a compound word is often related to the meanings of the individual characters. But this is not always the case, and sometimes the word takes on a new and very specific meaning. So to be able to read Chinese sentences and understand what they mean, it isn't enough just to learn individual characters—you'll also need to learn words. (In fact, many individual characters have very little meaning at all by themselves, and only take on meanings when paired with other characters).

Here are some examples of common Chinese words where the meaning of the overall word is not what you might expect from the meanings of the individual characters:

明		天		明天
míng	+	**tiān**	=	**míng tiān**
bright		day/sky		tomorrow

好		在		好在
hǎo	+	**zài**	=	**hǎo zài**
good		be present at/ live at		fortunately

If you think about it, the same thing happens in English. If you know what "battle" and "ship" mean, you can probably guess what a "battleship" might be. But this wouldn't work with "championship"! Similarly, you'd be unlikely to guess the meaning of "honeymoon" if you only knew the words "honey" and "moon".

The good news is that learning compound words can help you to learn the characters. For example, you may know (from your Chinese lessons) that **xīng qī** means "week". So when you see that this word is written 星期, you will know that 星 is pronounced **xīng**, and 期 is pronounced **qī**—even when these characters are forming part of *other* words. In fact, you will find that you remember many characters as half of some familiar word.

When you see a word written in characters, you can also often see how the word came to mean what it does. For example, **xīng qī** is 星期 which literally means "star period". This will help you to remember both the word *and* the two individual characters.

What is a stroke count?
Each Chinese character is made up of a number of pen or brush strokes. Each individual stroke is the mark made by a pen or brush before lifting it off the paper to write the next stroke. Strokes come in various shapes and sizes—a stroke can be a straight line, a curve, a bent line, a line with

a hook, or a dot. There is a traditional and very specific way that every character should be written. The order and direction of the strokes are both important if the character is to have the correct appearance.

What counts as a stroke is determined by tradition and is not always obvious. For example, the small box that often appears as part of a character (like the one on page 32, in the character 名) counts as three strokes, not four! (This is because a single stroke is traditionally used to write the top and right-hand sides of the box).

All this may sound rather pedantic but it is well worth learning how to write the characters correctly and with the correct number of strokes. One reason is that knowing how to count the strokes correctly is useful for looking up characters in dictionaries, as you'll see later.

This book shows you how to write characters stroke by stroke, and once you get the feel of it you'll very quickly learn how to work out the stroke count of a character you haven't met before, and get it right!

What are radicals?
Although the earliest characters were simple drawings, most characters are complex with two or more parts. And you'll find that some simple characters appear over and over again as parts of many complex characters. Have a look at these five characters:

她 she
妈 mother
姐 older sister
好 good
姓 surname

All five of these characters have the same component on the left-hand side: 女, which means "woman". This component gives a clue to the meaning of the character, and is called the "radical". As you can see, most of these five characters have something to do with the idea of "woman", but as you can also see, it's not a totally reliable way of guessing the meaning of a character. (Meanings of characters are something you just have to learn, without much help from their component parts).

Unfortunately the radical isn't always on the left-hand side of a character. Sometimes it's on the right, or on the top, or on the bottom. Here are some examples:

Character	Radical	Position of radical
都	阝	right
星	日	top
您	心	bottom
这	辶	left and bottom

Because it's not always easy to tell what the radical is for a particular character, it's given explicitly in a separate box for each of the characters in this book. However, as you learn more and more characters, you'll find that you can often guess the radical just by looking at a character.

Why bother with radicals? Well, for hundreds of years Chinese dictionaries have used the radical component of each character as a way of indexing them. All characters, even the really simple ones, are assigned to one radical or another so that they can be placed within the index of a Chinese dictionary (see the next section).

Incidentally, when you take away the radical, what's left is often a clue to the *pronunciation* of the character (this remainder is called the "phonetic component"). For example, 吗 and 妈 are formed by adding different radicals to the character 马 "horse" which is pronounced **mǎ**. Now 吗 is pronounced **ma** and 妈 is pronounced **ma**, so you can see that these two characters have inherited their pronunciations from the phonetic component 马. Unfortunately these "phonetic components" aren't very dependable: for example 也 on its own is pronounced **yě** but 他 and 她 are both pronounced **tā**.

How do I find a character in an index or a dictionary?
This is a question lots of people ask, and the answer varies according to the type of dictionary you are using. Many dictionaries today are organized alphabetically by pronunciation. So if you want to look up a character in a dictionary and you know its pronunciation, then it's easy. It's when you don't know the pronunciation of a character that there's a problem, since there is no alphabetical order for characters like there is for English words.

If you don't know the pronunciation of a character, then you will need to use a radical index (which is why radicals are useful). To use this you have to know which part of the character is the radical, and you will also need to be able to count the number of strokes that make up the character. To look up 姓, for example, 女 is the radical (which has 3 strokes) and the remaining part 生 has 5 strokes. So first you find the radical 女 amongst the 3-stroke radicals in the radical index. Then, since there are lots of characters under 女, look for 姓 in the section which lists all the 女 characters which have 5-stroke remainders.

This workbook has both a Hanyu Pinyin index and a radical index. Why not get used to how these indexes work by picking a character in the book and seeing if you can find it in both of the indexes?

Many dictionaries also have a pure stroke count index (i.e. ignoring the radical). This is useful if you cannot figure out what the radical of the character is. To use this you must count up all the strokes in the character as a whole and then look the character up under that number (so you would look up 姓 under 8 strokes). As you can imagine, this type of index can leave you with long columns of characters to scan through before you find the one you're looking for, so it's usually a last resort!

All these methods have their pitfalls and complications, so recently a completely new way of looking up characters has been devised. The *Chinese Character Fast Finder* (also by Tuttle Publishing) organizes characters purely by their shapes so that you can look up any one of 3,000 characters very quickly without knowing its meaning, radical, pronunciation or stroke count!

How should I use this workbook?
One good way to learn characters is to practice writing them, especially if you think about what each character means as you write it. This will fix the characters in your memory better than if you just look at them without writing them.

If you're working on your own without a teacher, work on a few characters at a time. Go at a pace that suits you; it's much better to do small but regular amounts of writing than to do large chunks at irregular intervals. You might start with just one or two characters each day and increase this as you get better at it. Frequent repetition is the key! Try to get into a daily routine of learning a few new characters and also reviewing the ones you learned on previous days. It's also a good idea to keep a list of which characters you've learned each day, and then to "test yourself" on the characters you learned the previous day, three days ago, a week ago and a month ago. Each time you test yourself they will stay in your memory for a longer period.

But *don't* worry if you can't remember a character you wrote out ten times only yesterday! This is quite normal to begin with. Just keep going—it will all be sinking in without you realizing it.

Once you've learned a few characters you can use flash cards to test yourself on them in a random order. You can make your own set of cards, or use a ready-made set like *Chinese in a Flash* (see the inside back cover).

How do I write the characters?
Finally, let's get down to business and talk about actually writing the characters! Under each character in this book, the first few boxes show how the character is written,

stroke by stroke. There is a correct way to draw each character, and the diagrams in the boxes show you both the order to draw the strokes in, and also the direction for each stroke.

Use the three gray examples to trace over and then carry on by yourself, drawing the characters using the correct stroke order and directions. The varying thicknesses of the lines show you what the characters would look like if they were drawn with a brush, but if you're using a pencil or ball-point pen don't worry about this. Just trace down the middle of the lines and you will produce good hand-written characters.

Pay attention to the length of each of the strokes so that your finished character has the correct proportions. Use the gray dotted lines inside each box as a guide to help you start and end each stroke in the right place.

You may think that it doesn't really matter how the strokes are written as long as the end result looks the same. To some extent this is true, but there are some good reasons for knowing the "proper" way to write the characters. Firstly, it helps you to count strokes, and secondly it will make your finished character "look right", and also help you to read other people's hand-written characters later on. It's better in the long run to learn the correct method of writing the characters from the beginning because, as with so many other things, once you get into "bad" habits it can be very hard to break them!

If you are left-handed, just use your left hand as normal, but still make sure you use the correct stroke order and directions when writing the strokes. For example, draw your horizontal strokes left to right, even if it feels more natural to draw them right to left.

For each Chinese character there is a fixed, correct order in which to write the strokes. But these "stroke orders" do follow some fairly general rules. The main thing to remember is:
- Generally work left to right and top to bottom.

Some other useful guidelines are:
- Horizontal lines are written before vertical ones (see 十, page 19);
- Lines that slope down and to the left are written before those that slope down and to the right (see 文, page 41);
- A central part or vertical line is written before symmetrical or smaller lines at the sides (see 小, page 47);
- The top and sides of an outer box are written first, then whatever is inside the box, then the bottom is written last to "close" it (see 国, page 56).

As you work through the book you'll see these rules in action and get a feel for them, and you'll know how to draw virtually any Chinese character without having to be shown.

Practice, practice, practice!
Your first attempts at writing will be awkward, but as with most things you'll get better with practice. That's why there are lots of squares for you to use. And don't be too hard on yourself (we all draw clumsy-looking characters when we start); just give yourself plenty of time and practice. After a while, you'll be able to look back at your early attempts and compare them with your most recent ones, and see just how much you've improved.

After writing the same character a number of times (a row or two at most), move on to another one. Don't fill up the whole page at one sitting! Then, after writing several other characters, come back later and do a few more of the first one. Can you remember the stroke order without having to look at the diagram?

Finally, try writing out sentences, or lines of different characters, on ordinary paper. To begin with you can mark out squares to write in if you want to, but after that simply imagine the squares and try to keep your characters all equally sized and equally spaced.

Have fun, and remember—the more you practice writing the characters the easier it gets!

		common words				1 stroke	

一 **yī** one; single; a(n)

common words

一个 **yí ge** a(n); one (of something)
一次 **yí cì** once
一同／一起 **yī tóng/yī qǐ** together
一月 **yí yuè** January
十一 **shí yī** eleven
第一 **dì yī** first
星期一 **xīng qī yī** Monday

1 stroke

radical

一

二

èr two (number)

common words		2 strokes
		radical
		一

二十　**èr shí**　twenty
二妹　**èr mèi**　second younger sister
二月　**èr yuè**　February
二手　**èr shǒu**　secondhand (adj.)
十二　**shí èr**　twelve
第二　**dì èr**　second
星期二　**xīng qī èr**　Tuesday

三

sān three

radical

一

common words

三十　**sān shí**　thirty
三月　**sān yuè**　March
三个月　**sān ge yuè**　three months
三明治　**sān míng zhì**　sandwich
十三　**shí sān**　thirteen
第三　**dì sān**　third
星期三　**xīng qī sān**　Wednesday

四

sì four

common words

四十　**sì shí**　forty
四百　**sì bǎi**　four hundred
四月　**sì yuè**　April
四处　**sì chù**　everywhere
十四　**shí sì**　fourteen
第四　**dì sì**　fourth
星期四　**xīng qī sì**　Thursday

丨	冂	冈	四	四	四	四	四

五

wǔ five

common words

五十　**wǔ shí**　fifty
五月　**wǔ yuè**　May
五年　**wǔ nián**　five years
五本　**wǔ běn**　five (books)
十五　**shí wǔ**　fifteen
第五　**dì wǔ**　fifth
星期五　**xīng qī wǔ**　Friday

一　丆　五　五　五　五　五

六

liù six

common words

六十三 **liù shí sān** sixty-three
六月 **liù yuè** June
六个月 **liù ge yuè** six months
六天 **liù tiān** six days
十六 **shí liù** sixteen
第六 **dì liù** sixth
星期六 **xīng qī liù** Saturday

七

qī seven

common words

七十七　**qī shí qī**　seventy-seven

七百　**qī bǎi**　seven hundred

七月　**qī yuè**　July

十七　**shí qī**　seventeen

七七八八　**qī qī bā bā**　almost complete

七上八下　**qī shàng bā xià**　worry; anxious

第七　**dì qī**　seventh

一　七　七　七　七

八

bā eight

common words

八十二 **bā shí èr** eighty-two
八百零五 **bā bǎi líng wǔ** eight-hundred and five
八月 **bā yuè** August
八成 **bā chéng** 80 per cent
八折 **bā zhé** 20 per cent discount
十八 **shí bā** eighteen
第八 **dì bā** eighth

九

jiǔ nine

common words

九十八　**jiǔ shí bā**　ninety-eight
九百一十　**jiǔ bǎi yí shí**　nine-hundred and ten
九月　**jiǔ yuè**　September
九号　**jiǔ hào**　number/size nine; ninth (of a month)
九分　**jiǔ fēn**　nine points
十九　**shí jiǔ**　nineteen
第九　**dì jiǔ**　ninth

2 strokes

radical

丿

丿　九　九　九　九

18

十	common words	2 strokes

shí ten

common words

十月 **shí yuè** October
十一月 **shí yī yuè** November
十二月 **shí èr yuè** December
十分 **shí fēn** 1. ten points 2. very
十全十美 **shí quán shí měi** perfect; ideal
第十 **dì shí** tenth

2 strokes

radical

十

一	十	十	十	十			

你

nǐ you

common words

你好　**nǐ hǎo**　How do you do?
你的　**nǐ de**　your; yours
你们　**nǐ men**　you (plural)
你们的　**nǐ men de**　your; yours (plural)

7 strokes

radical

人（亻）

亻¹　亻²　亻³　你⁴　你⁵　你⁶　你⁷　你

你　你

您

nín you (polite)

common words

您好 **nín hǎo** How do you do? (polite)

您早 **nín zǎo** Good morning!

您贵姓？ **nín guì xìng** your family name?

11 strokes

radical

心

好

hǎo/hào 1. good
2. alright 3. like

common words

好啊! **hǎo a** Good!; OK!
好看 **hǎo kàn** 1. good show 2. good looking
好久 **hǎo jiǔ** a long time
很好 **hěn hǎo** very good
还好 **hái hǎo** still alright
那好 **nà hǎo** alright then ... (agreeing to a suggestion)
爱好 **ài hào** hobby, interest in something

6 strokes

radical

女

请

qǐng 1. please
2. to invite

common words

请问 **qǐng wèn** May I ask ...?
请坐 **qǐng zuò** Please sit down.
请进 **qǐng jìn** Please come in.
请客 **qǐng kè** play host; treat
请教 **qǐng jiào** seek advice
请假 **qǐng jià** take leave

10 strokes

radical

讠

traditional form

請

问

wèn ask

问好 **wèn hǎo** say hello to...
问题 **wèn tí** question; problem
问答 **wèn dá** question and answer
学问 **xué wèn** knowledge
访问 **fǎng wèn** 1. visit 2. interview

6 strokes

radical

门

traditional form

問

		common words				**9 strokes**
贵		贵姓 **guì xìng** your honorable surname? 贵人 **guì rén** respected person 贵客/贵宾 **guì kè/guì bīn** distinguished guest; VIP 太贵了 **tài guì le** too expensive 名贵 **míng guì** valuable				**radical** 贝
guì 1. honorable 2. expensive; valuable						**traditional form** 貴

｜	冖	口	中	虫	串	青	贵
贵	贵	贵	贵				

姓

xìng surname

姓名 **xìng míng** full name
同姓 **tóng xìng** having the same surname
老百姓 **lǎo bǎi xìng** common people

8 strokes

radical

女

丨 女 女 女 女 女 女 姓

姓 姓 姓

他

tā he

common words

他的 **tā de** his
他们 **tā men** they; them (male)
他们的 **tā men de** their; theirs (male)
他人／其他人 **tā rén/qí tā rén** other people
其他 **qí tā** other

radical

人（亻）

丿	亻	仴	伷	他	他	他	他

她	common words	6 strokes
tā she	她的 **tā de** hers 她们 **tā men** they; them (female) 她们的 **tā men de** their; theirs (female)	radical 女

叫

jiào 1. call; be called
2. shout 3. order

common words

叫门 **jiào mén** call at the door
叫好 **jiào hǎo** cheer
叫喊 **jiào hǎn** shout; yell
叫做 **jiào zuò** be called
叫车 **jiào chē** order a cab
大叫 **dà jiào** call out loudly

5 strokes

radical

口

什

shén/shí 1. mixed
2. tenth (mathematics)

common words

什么 **shén me** what
什么的 **shén me de** etc; so on...
什么时候? **shén me shí hòu** when?; at what time?

4 strokes

radical

人（亻）

丿	亻	仁	什	什	什	什	

30

么

me interrogative particle

common words

什么 **shén me** what
怎么 **zěn me** how
那么 **nà me** in that way; so...
多么 **duō me** no matter how
为什么? **wèi shén me** why?

3 strokes

radical
ㄙ

traditional form

麼

名

míng 1. name
2. fame

common words

名字 **míng zi** name
名叫 **míng jiào** named
名人 **míng rén** celebrity; famous person
同名 **tóng míng** having the same name
出名 **chū míng** become famous; well-known
第一名 **dì yī míng** first in position

字

字母 **zì mǔ** letter (alphabet)
字典 **zì diǎn** dictionary
十字 **shí zì** cross
汉字 **hàn zì** Chinese (Han) character
写字 **xiě zì** write word
生字 **shēng zì** new word

6 strokes

radical

宀

zì written character

字

33

我

wǒ I; me

radical

戈

common words

我的 **wǒ de** my; mine
我们 **wǒ men** we; us
我国 **wǒ guó** our country
我家 **wǒ jiā** my family; my home
自我 **zì wǒ** self

是

shì to be; yes

是的 **shì de** yes
是啊 **shì a** yes; yeah
是不是 **shì bu shì** to be or not to be
不是 **bú shi** 1. not to be; no 2. fault
还是 **hái shì** or
老是 **lǎo shì** always

9 strokes

radical

日

丨	冂	日	日	旦	旱	旱	是
是	是	是	是				

大

dà big; great

common words

大声点 **dà shēng diǎn** louder
大家 **dà jiā** everybody
大不了 **dà bu liǎo** at the worst
大多／大都／大半 **dà duō/dà dū/dà bàn** mostly
大小 **dà xiǎo** size
大概 **dà gài** probably
自大 **zì dà** proud; arrogant

一 ナ 大 大 大 大

学

xué learn

common words

学会 **xué huì** learned; mastered
学习 **xué xí** study
上学 **shàng xué** go to school
放学 **fàng xué** finish school for the day
开学 **kāi xué** school reopens
小学 **xiǎo xué** primary school
中学 **zhōng xué** middle/secondary school

8 strokes

radical
子

traditional form
學

生

shēng 1. give birth; born 2. raw

common words

生日　**shēng rì**　birthday
生气　**shēng qì**　angry
生病　**shēng bìng**　fall sick; not well
生吃　**shēng chī**　eat raw food
学生　**xué sheng**　student
先生　**xiān sheng**　1. Mr 2. husband
医生　**yī shēng**　doctor

丿¹　ⵑ²　乍³　牛⁴　生⁵　生　生　生

		common words		4 strokes	

中

zhōng/zhòng 1. among 2. (in the) course 3. hit by

common words

中国　**zhōng guó**　China
中文　**zhōng wén**　Chinese language (written)
中间　**zhōng jiān**　between; in the middle
中年　**zhōng nián**　middle-aged
中奖　**zhòng jiǎng**　win a prize
心中　**xīn zhōng**　in one's heart
手中　**shǒu zhōng**　on hand

4 strokes

radical

丨

丨	冂	口	中	中	中	中	

英

yīng 1. related to England 2. hero

common words

英国 **yīng guó** England
英文 **yīng wén** English language (written)
英语 **yīng yǔ** English language
英俊 **yīng jùn** handsome
英明 **yīng míng** wise
英雄 **yīng xióng** hero

8 strokes

radical
艹

文

wén written language; writing

common words		4 strokes
文字 **wén zì** script; writing		**radical**
文具 **wén jù** stationery		文
文学 **wén xué** literature		
语文 **yǔ wén** language (spoken and written)		
法文 **fǎ wén** French (written)		
日文 **rì wén** Japanese (written)		

课

kè lesson; class

radical
讠

traditional form
課

common words

课本　**kè běn**　textbook
课题　**kè tí**　topic (of lessons)
课文　**kè wén**　text
上课　**shàng kè**　attend class
下课　**xià kè**　finish class
功课　**gōng kè**　homework
第一课　**dì yī kè**　first lesson; lesson one

丶	讠	讠	讠	讠	讠	讠
课	课	课	课	课		

老

lǎo old

common words

老师　**lǎo shī**　teacher

老大　**lǎo dà**　1. eldest sibling 2. gang leader

老婆　**lǎo po**　wife (informal)

老公　**lǎo gōng**　husband (informal)

老婆婆　**lǎo pó po**　old woman

老外　**lǎo wài**　foreigner

古老　**gǔ lǎo**　ancient

二	十	土	少	耂	老	老	老
老							

师

shī teacher; master

radical
巾

traditional form
師

common words

师生 **shī shēng** teacher and student
师父 **shī fu** master
老师/教师 **lǎo shī/jiào shī** teacher
律师 **lǜ shī** lawyer
厨师 **chú shī** chef

丨	刂	厂	师	师	师	师	师
师							

同

tóng the same; together

common words

同学 **tóng xué** classmate
同班 **tóng bān** same class
同时 **tóng shí** at the same time
同样 **tóng yàng** the same; alike
同事 **tóng shì** colleague
一同／一起 **yī tóng/yī qǐ** together

6 strokes

radical

冂

丨	冂	同	同	同	同	同	同
同							

校

xiào school

校长　**xiào zhǎng**　principal
校服　**xiào fú**　school uniform
校友　**xiào yǒu**　schoolmate; alumni
学校　**xué xiào**　school
同校　**tóng xiào**　same school
上校　**shàng xiào**　colonel

10 strokes

radical

木

一　十　才　木　术　朾　栌　校

栌　校　校　校　校

46

小

xiǎo small; little

radical

小（⺍）

common words

小姐　**xiǎo jiě**　Miss; lady
小时　**xiǎo shí**　hour
小时候　**xiǎo shí hou**　in one's childhood
小心　**xiǎo xīn**　(be) careful
小看　**xiǎo kàn**　belittle; underestimate
小便　**xiǎo biàn**　urine; urinate

亅　小　小　小　小　小

朋

péng friend

radical

月

common words

朋友 **péng you** friend
好朋友 **hǎo péng you** good friend
男朋友 **nán péng you** boyfriend
女朋友 **nǚ péng you** girlfriend
老朋友 **lǎo péng you** old friend
小朋友 **xiǎo péng you** kid; child

友

yǒu friend

common words
友人 **yǒu rén** friend
友谊/友情 **yǒu yì/yǒu qíng** friendship
好友 **hǎo yǒu** good friend
男友 **nán yǒu** boyfriend
女友 **nǚ yǒu** girlfriend
工友 **gōng yǒu** fellow worker; caretaker

radical

又

一 ナ 方 友 友 友 友

们

men plural suffix
(for persons)

common words

你们 **nǐ men** you (plural)
我们／咱们 **wǒ men/zán men** we; us
女士们 **nǚ shì men** ladies
男士们 **nán shì men** gentlemen
同学们 **tóng xué men** classmates
人们 **rén men** people

5 strokes

radical

人（亻）

traditional form

們

亻	亻	亻	们	们	们	们	们

呢

ne question particle

common words

你呢? **nǐ ne** How about you?

他（她）呢? **tā ne** How about him (her)?

我们呢? **wǒ men ne** How about us?

人呢? **rén ne** Where's the person?

丨	口	口	口	口	呎	呢	呢

呢	呢	呢					

谢

xiè thank

谢谢 **xiè xie** thank you
谢词 **xiè cí** thank you speech
多谢 **duō xiè** many thanks
不谢 **bú xiè** don't mention it
答谢 **dá xiè** express appreciation

12 strokes
radical
讠
traditional form
謝

丶	讠	讠	讠	词	讵	讷	谢
谢	谢	谢	谢	谢	谢	谢	

再

zài again

common words

再见／再会 **zài jiàn/zài huì** Goodbye!

再三 **zài sān** again and again; repeatedly

再次 **zài cì** once more

再不 **zài bu** or; or else

一再 **yí zài** again and again; repeatedly

不再 **bú zài** no longer; never again

见

jiàn see; meet

radical

见

traditional form

見

common words

见好 **jiàn hǎo** get better (from an illness)
见面 **jiàn miàn** meet
不见了 **bú jiàn le** missing; can't be found
不见得 **bú jiàn de** not necessarily
看见 **kàn jiàn** see
少见 **shǎo jiàn** rare
听见 **tīng jiàn** hear

美

měi beautiful

radical

羊（ 羊 ）

common words

美丽 **měi lì** beautiful; pretty
美好 **měi hǎo** wonderful
美食 **měi shí** culinary delicacy, gourmet food
美女／美人 **měi nǚ/měi rén** beautiful girl/woman
美国 **měi guó** the Unites States of America
很美／太美了 **hěn měi/tài měi le** very beautiful

丷	丷	丷	丷	丷	丷	美
美	美	美	美			

国

guó country; national

common words

国家 **guó jiā** country
国民 **guó mín** people of a country
国王 **guó wáng** king
出国 **chū guó** go abroad
外国 **wài guó** foreign country
外国人 **wài guó rén** people from another country,
　　foreigners

8 strokes

radical

口

traditional form

國

人

rén person; people

common words

人人／每人 **rén rén/měi rén** everyone
人口 **rén kǒu** population
工人 **gōng rén** worker
大人／成人 **dà rén/chéng rén** adult
本人 **běn rén** oneself
客人 **kè rén** guest

2 strokes

radical

人

丿 人 人 人 人

吗

ma question particle

common words

是吗？ **shì ma** Is that so?; Is it?
好吗？ **hǎo ma** good?; alright?
忙吗？ **máng ma** busy?
行吗？ **xíng ma** Is it okay?
可以吗？ **kě yǐ ma** May I?
有事吗？ **yǒu shì ma** what's up?

6 strokes

radical

口

traditional form

嗎

丨	口	口	吗	吗	吗	吗	吗
吗							

也

yě also; too

common words

也是 **yě shì** is also ...
也好 **yě hǎo** may as well
也许 **yě xǔ** perhaps

也 也 也 也 也 也

59

不

bù not; no

common words

不对 **bú duì** 1. incorrect 2. something is wrong
不要 **bú yào** don't want
不会 **bú huì** 1. don't know how 2. unlikely
不同/不一样 **bù tóng/bù yí yàng** it's different
不客气 **bú kè qi** not at all; don't mention it
不好意思 **bù hǎo yì si** 1. embarrassed 2. excuse me
对不起 **duì bu qǐ** sorry

一 丆 丆 不 不 不 不

谁

shéi/shuí who

common words

谁的 **shéi de/shuí de** whose
谁知道 **shéi zhī dào/shuí zhī dào** no one knows

10 strokes

radical

讠

traditional form

誰

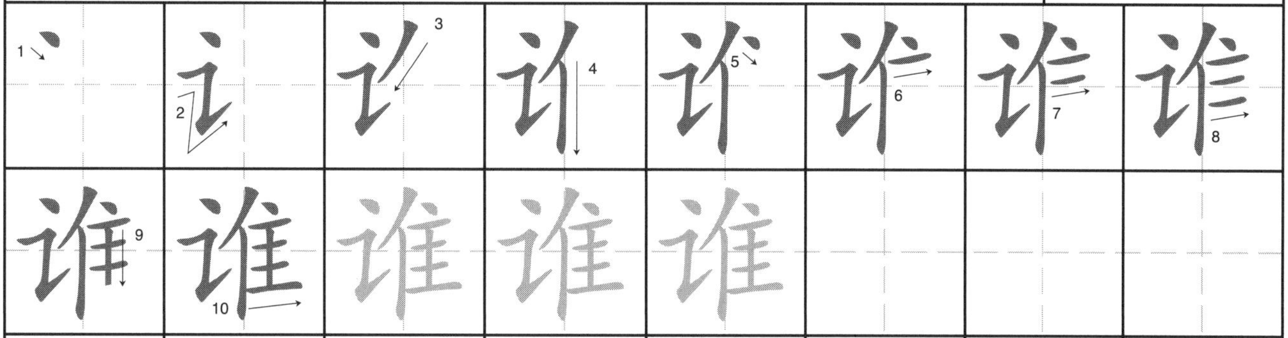

的

de particle

common words

我的 **wǒ de** my; mine
你的 **nǐ de** your; yours
他的/她的 **tā de** his/hers
谁的 **shéi de/shuí de** whose
有的 **yǒu de** some
挺好的 **tǐng hǎo de** quite good

家

jiā family; home

common words

家庭 **jiā tíng** family
家人 **jiā rén** family member
人家 **rén jiā** other people
回家 **huí jiā** return home
每家/家家 **měi jiā/jiā jiā** every family; every household
一家大小 **yī jiā dà xiǎo** everyone in a family

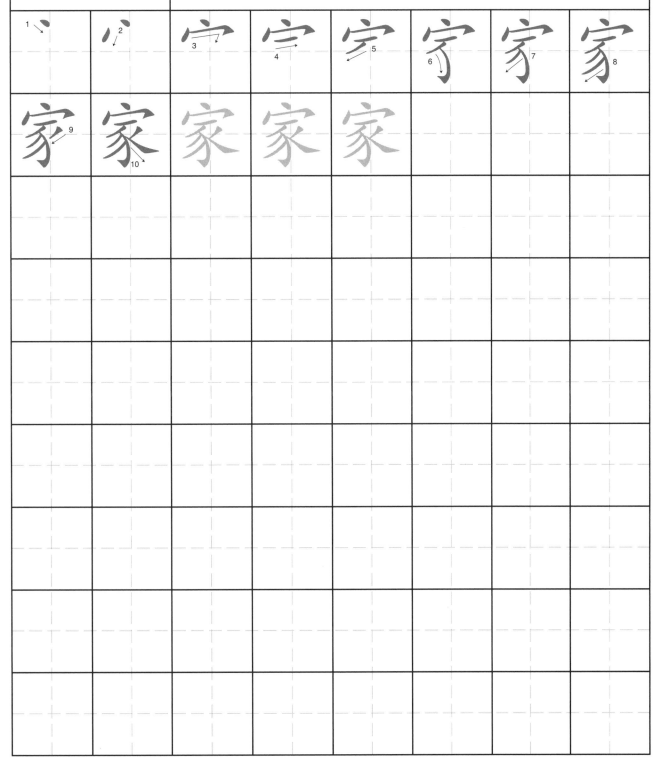

bà father

common words

爸爸 **bà ba** father
爸爸妈妈 **bà ba mā ma** parents
老爸 **lǎo bà** father (informal)

8 strokes

radical

父

和

hé 1. ...and...
2. harmony

common words

和好 **hé hǎo** reconcile
和气 **hé qì** amiable; friendly
和平 **hé píng** peace
和事老 **hé shì lǎo** mediator

8 strokes

radical

禾

二	二	千	禾	禾	和	和	和
和	和	和					

妈

mā mother

妈妈 **mā ma** mother
姨妈 **yí mā** aunt (mother's married sister)
姑妈 **gū mā** aunt (father's married sister)

6 strokes

radical

女

traditional form

媽

哥

gē older brother

common words		10 strokes
哥哥 **gē ge** older brother		**radical**
大哥 **dà gē** eldest brother		一
二哥 **èr gē** second elder brother		
哥儿们 **gēr men** 1. brothers 2. buddies		
帅哥 **shuài gē** handsome man		

姐

jiě older sister

radical

女

common words

姐姐 **jiě jie** older sister
姐妹 **jiě mèi** sisters
大姐 **dà jiě** 1. eldest sister 2. older woman
二姐 **èr jiě** second elder sister
小姐 **xiǎo jiě** Miss; lady
空姐 **kōng jiě** air stewardess

乀	女	女	如	如	姐	姐	姐
姐	姐	姐					

68

弟

dì younger brother

common words

弟弟 **dì di** younger brother

弟妹 **dì mèi** 1. younger brother and sister 2. younger brother's wife

兄弟 **xiōng dì** brothers

姐弟 **jiě dì** older sister and younger brother

徒弟 **tú dì** disciple; follower

7 strokes

radical

八（丷）

妹

mèi younger sister

common words

妹妹 **mèi mei** younger sister
大妹 **dà mèi** first younger sister
三妹 **sān mèi** third younger sister
小妹 **xiǎo mèi** youngest sister
姐妹 **jiě mèi** sisters
兄弟姐妹 **xiōng dì jiě mèi** brothers and sisters

8 strokes

radical

女

70

住

zhù 1. live; stay
2. stop

radical

人（亻）

common words

住家　**zhù jiā**　residence
住址　**zhù zhǐ**　address (residence)
住口　**zhù kǒu**　shut up
住手　**zhù shǒu**　Hands off!
站住　**zhàn zhù**　Halt!
记住　**jì zhù**　remember

在

zài 1. be; at 2. live

radical

土

common words

在吗? **zài ma** in?
在家里 **zài jiā lǐ** at home
不在 **bú zài** not in
现在 **xiàn zài** now; currently
还在 **hái zài** still there
好在 **hǎo zài** fortunately

一　ナ　オ　右　在　在　在

在

72

这
zhè this

common words			7 strokes

common words

这个 **zhè ge** 1. this one 2. in this case; in this matter
这儿/这里/这边 **zhèr/zhè lǐ/zhè biān** here
这些 **zhè xiē** these
这样 **zhè yàng** this way; like this
这么 **zhè me** such, so
这次 **zhè cì** this time
到这儿来 **dào zhèr lái** Come here!

radical

辶

traditional form

這

73

女

nǚ female

common words

女儿 **nǚ ér** daughter
女生 **nǚ shēng** female student; school girl
女性 **nǚ xìng** female gender
女士 **nǚ shì** Madam
女人 **nǚ rén** 1. woman 2. wife 3. mistress
妇女 **fù nǚ** woman

儿

ér/r 1. child 2. suffix

common words

儿子 **ér zi** son
儿童 **ér tóng** child
大儿子 **dà ér zi** eldest son
小儿子 **xiǎo ér zi** youngest son
一会儿 **yí huìr** a moment; a short while
一点儿 **yì diǎnr** a little

2 strokes

radical

儿

traditional form

兒

儿 儿 儿 儿 儿

那

nà/nèi 1. that
2. in that case

common words

那个 **nà ge** that (one)
那里／那儿／那边 **nà li/nàr/nà biān** there
那些 **nà xiē** those
那样 **nà yàng** 1. same as 2. that type
那么 **nà me** 1. in that case; then 2. same way
那么点儿 **nà me diǎnr** such a small amount ...

刁	刁	刁	刭	那	那	那	那
那							

男

nán male

common words

男孩／男孩子 **nán hái/nán hái zi** boy
男生 **nán shēng** male student; school boy
男人 **nán rén** man
男性 **nán xìng** male gender
男男女女 **nán nán nǚ nǚ** boys and girls
男厕／男厕所 **nán cè/nán cè suǒ** man's toilet

孩

hái child

孩子/小孩 **hái zi/xiǎo hái** child
孩子气 **hái zi qì** childish
孩子话 **hái zi huà** childish words
男孩/男孩子 **nán hái/nán hái zi** boy
女孩/女孩子 **nǚ hái/nǚ hái zi** girl

9 strokes

radical

子

子

zi/zǐ 1. son 2. seed
3. suffix (noun)

common words

子女／儿女 **zǐ nǚ/ér nǚ** son and daughter; children
儿子 **ér zi** son
妻子 **qī zi** wife
桌子 **zhuō zi** table; desk
车子 **chē zi** 1. vehicle (small scale) 2. bicycle
一下子 **yí xià zi** 1. all of a sudden 2. all at once

3 strokes

radical

子

都

dōu/dū 1. all; even
2. big city

common words

都有　**dōu yǒu**　all have
都是　**dōu shì**　all are
都会　**dōu huì**　all know how to do
都市/都会　**dū shì/dū huì**　big city
首都　**shǒu dū**　capital city

一	十	土	尹	者	者	者	者
者	都	都	都	都			

没

méi haven't; without

common words

没有 **méi yǒu** don't have; haven't
没错 **méi cuò** correct
没问题 **méi wèn tí** no question; no problem
没事 **méi shì** 1. free 2. no problem; alright
没关系/没什么 **méi guān xi/méi shén me**
it doesn't matter
还没 **hái méi** not yet

7 strokes

radical

氵

traditional form

没

有

yǒu has; have

有的/有些 **yǒu de/yǒu xiē** some
有学问 **yǒu xué wèn** knowledgeable
有点儿 **yǒu diǎnr** a little; somewhat
有没有(?) **yǒu méi yǒu** 1. did you? 2. whether or not
只有 **zhǐ yǒu** there's only ...
还有 **hái yǒu** moreover; furthermore

一 ナ 才 有 有 有 有 有

有

做

zuò do; make

common words

做好/做完 **zuò hǎo/zuò wán** finish; complete
做错 **zuò cuò** do wrongly
做人 **zuò rén** be an upright person
做饭 **zuò fàn** cook a meal
做作业 **zuò zuò yè** do assignment
做工 **zuò gōng** work

11 strokes

radical

人（亻）

事

shì matter

common words

事事／每事 **shì shì/měi shì** every matter
事前 **shì qián** in advance; beforehand
事后 **shì hòu** afterwards; after the event
小事 **xiǎo shì** trivial matter
故事 **gù shì** story
做事 **zuò shì** 1. work 2. deal with matters

8 strokes

radical

一

一	丁	丂	亏	亐	亖	亖	事
事	事	事					

两

liǎng two

两个月 **liǎng ge yuè** two months
两百 **liǎng bǎi** two hundred
两次 **liǎng cì** twice
两样 **liǎng yàng** two types; different
两口子 **liǎng kǒu zi** a couple; husband and wife
没两样 **méi liǎng yàng** the same

7 strokes

radical

一

traditional form

兩

85

个

gè most common measure word

		3 strokes
		radical 人
		traditional form 個

common words

个个/每个 **gè gè/měi ge** each one (of something)
个人 **gè rén** individual
个子 **gè zi** body size
两个门 **liǎng ge mén** two doors
那个 **nà ge** that (one)
这个 **zhè ge** 1. this one 2. in this case; in this matter

ノ¹	个²	个³	个	个	个		

多

duō 1. many, much
2. far more

| | common words | | | | | | 6 strokes |
| | | | | | | | radical 夕 |

多少(?) **duō shǎo** 1. how many/much? 2. tend to
多大(?) **duō dà** 1. how old(?) 2. how big(?)
多半 **duō bàn** more often than not
多么 **duō me** no matter how
差不多 **chà bu duō** about; more or less

丿	夕	夕	夕	多	多	多	多
多							

少

shǎo/shào 1. few; little 2. young

radical

小

common words

少女 **shào nǚ** teenage girl
少不了 **shǎo bu liǎo** can't do without
青少年 **qīng shào nián** teenager
很少 **hěn shǎo** very little; very few
不少 **bù shǎo** quite a lot
男女老少 **nán nǚ lǎo shào** men, women, young and old

少　少　少　少　少　少

时

shí time

common words

时间 **shí jiān** time
时期 **shí qī** period of time
时时／不时 **shí shí/bù shí** often
一时 **yī shí** temporarily; momentarily
有时／有时候 **yǒu shí/yǒu shí hou** sometimes
到时 **dào shí** when the time comes

7 strokes

radical

日

traditional form

時

89

间

jiān 1. between 2. room 3. measure word

common words

时间 **shí jiān** time
中间 **zhōng jiān** between; in the middle
房间 **fáng jiān** room
夜间 **yè jiān** at night; night time
洗手间 **xǐ shǒu jiān** washroom
一间客房 **yī jiān kè fáng** a guest room

7 strokes

radical

门

traditional form

間

90

今

jīn now; at present

common words

今天／今日　**jīn tiān/jīn rì** today
今早　**jīn zǎo** this morning
今晚　**jīn wǎn** tonight; this evening
今年　**jīn nián** this year
今后　**jīn hòu** from now on
至今　**zhì jīn** up to now; so far
如今　**rú jīn** now; nowadays

4 strokes

radical

人

ノ	人	仌	今	今	今	今	

天

tiān 1. day 2. sky

common words

天天/每天 **tiān tiān/měi tiān** every day
天上/天空中 **tiān shàng/tiān kōng zhōng** in the sky
天气 **tiān qì** weather
明天 **míng tiān** tomorrow
昨天 **zuó tiān** yesterday
白天 **bái tiān** daytime

4 strokes

radical

大

一　二　开　天　天　天　天

92

几

jǐ/jī 1. how many
2. several 3. almost

common words

几个(?) **jǐ ge** 1. how many? 2. several (of something)
几次(?) **jǐ cì** 1. how many times? 2. several times
几时(?) **jǐ shí** 1. when? 2. anytime
几天(?) **jǐ tiān** 1. how many days? 2. several days
几分(?) **jǐ fēn** 1. how many points? 2. somewhat
几点(?) **jǐ diǎn** 1. what time? 2. several dots
几乎 **jī hū** almost, nearly

2 strokes

radical

几

traditional form

幾

丿　几　几　几　几

号

hào 1. date 2. size 3. sequence 4. signal

common words

号码 **hào mǎ** number
几号? **jǐ hào** which number?; what size?; what date?
十号 **shí hào** number ten; size ten; tenth (of a month)
句号 **jù hào** full-stop
逗号 **dòu hào** comma
问号 **wèn hào** question mark

5 strokes

radical

口

traditional form

號

丨	口	口	므	号	号	号	号

明

míng bright

common words

明明 **míng míng** obviously
明白 **míng bai** understand
明天／明日 **míng tiān/míng rì** tomorrow
明亮 **míng liàng** bright
文明 **wén míng** civilized; civilization
发明 **fā míng** invent

丨	冂	日	日	朙	明	明	明
明	明	明					

年

nián year

common words

年年/每年　**nián nián/měi nián** every year
年纪　**nián ji** age
明年　**míng nián** next year
后年　**hòu nián** year after next year
去年　**qù nián** last year
前年　**qián nián** year before last year

6 strokes

radical

丿

年

96

月

yuè 1. month 2. moon

common words

月亮／月球 **yuè liang/yuè qiú** moon
月光 **yuè guāng** moonlight
这个月 **zhè ge yuè** this month
上个月 **shàng ge yuè** last month
下个月 **xià ge yuè** next month

4 strokes

radical

月

月 月 月 月 月 月 月

日

rì day

common words

日本 **rì běn** Japan
日期 **rì qī** date
日子 **rì zi** 1. date; day 2. time 3. life
今日 **jīn rì** today
明日 **míng rì** tomorrow
昨日 **zuó rì** yesterday
每日 **měi rì** every day

4 strokes

radical

日

98

星

xīng star

common words

星星 **xīng xing** star
星期 **xīng qī** week
星座 **xīng zuó** 1. constellation 2. sign of zodiac
星球 **xīng qiú** heavenly body; planet
歌星 **gē xīng** singer
明星 **míng xīng** star (celebrity)

9 strokes

radical

日

⺊	冂	曰	日	旦	星	星	星

星	星	星	星				

期

qī period

12 strokes

radical

月

common words

期间／时期　**qī jiān/shí qī** period of time
学期　**xué qī** school term; semester
假期　**jià qī** holiday
到期　**dào qī** expire
早期　**zǎo qī** earlier time; early stage
上星期　**shàng xīng qī** last week
下星期　**xià xīng qī** next week

早

zǎo early; morning; Good morning!

common words

早安　**zǎo ān**　Good morning!
早上　**zǎo shang**　morning
早日　**zǎo rì**　(at an) early date; soon
早晚　**zǎo wǎn**　1. day and night 2. sooner or later
早饭/早点/早餐　**zǎo fàn/zǎo diǎn/zǎo cān**　breakfast
一早　**yī zǎo**　early in the morning
明早　**míng zǎo**　tomorrow morning

丨	冂	日	旦	旦	早	早	早
早							

上

shàng 1. above; go up
2. attend 3. previous

common words

上面 **shàng mian** above; top
上来 **shàng lái** come up
上去 **shàng qù** go up
上班 **shàng bān** go to work
上厕所 **shàng cè suǒ** go to the toilet
上次 **shàng cì** last time
马上 **mǎ shàng** immediately

3 strokes

radical

卜

下

xià 1. under; go down 2. finish 3. next

common words

下面 **xià mian** underneath; below
下来 **xià lái** come down
下去 **xià qù** go down
下班 **xià bān** finish work
下雨 **xià yǔ** rain
下次 **xià cì** next time
一下 **yí xià** 1. one time 2. a short while

3 strokes

radical
一

一	下	下	下	下	下		

午

wǔ noon

radical

十

common words

午饭/午餐 **wǔ fàn/wǔ cān** lunch

午觉/午睡 **wǔ jiào/wǔ shuì** afternoon nap

午夜 **wǔ yè** midnight

上午/午前 **shàng wǔ/wǔ qián** morning (a.m.)

中午 **zhōng wǔ** noon

下午/午后 **xià wǔ/wǔ hòu** afternoon (p.m.)

ノ ⠂ ⠂ 午 午 午 午

吃

chī eat

吃饭　**chī fàn**　have a meal
吃饱了　**chī bǎo le**　eaten; eaten enough
吃不饱　**chī bu bǎo**　not full; not enough to eat
吃不下　**chī bu xià**　not able to eat; have no appetite
小吃　**xiǎo chī**　snack
好吃　**hǎo chī**　tasty; delicious

6 strokes

radical

口

晚

wǎn night; late

common words

晚上 **wǎn shang** evening; night
晚安 **wǎn ān** Good night!
晚饭/晚餐 **wǎn fàn/wǎn cān** dinner
晚班 **wǎn bān** evening shift; night shift
晚点 **wǎn diǎn** be late
起晚了 **qǐ wǎn le** got up late

11 strokes

radical

日

丨	刂	日	日	日	旷	昣	晚
晚	晚	晚	晚	晚	晚		

饭

fàn meal; cooked rice

common words

饭前 **fàn qián** before a meal
饭后 **fàn hòu** after a meal
饭菜 **fàn cài** rice and dishes
饭店 **fàn diàn** 1. restaurant 2. hotel
白饭 **bái fàn** cooked white rice
开饭 **kāi fàn** start serving a meal

7 strokes

radical
饣

traditional form
飯

了

le/liǎo particle

common words

了不起 **liǎo bu qǐ** fantastic; amazing
对了 **duì le** That's right!
算了 **suàn le** forget it
都上学了 **dōu shàng xué le** all have gone to school
受不了 **shòu bu liǎo** unbearable
吃了 **chī le** had eaten

2 strokes

radical

一

了 了 了 了 了

108

哪

nǎ/něi which; any

radical

口

common words

哪个(?) **nǎ ge** 1. which? 2. any; anyone
哪里(?) **nǎ li** 1. where? 2. not at all
哪样(?) **nǎ yàng** 1. what kind? 2. whatever
哪天(?) **nǎ tiān** 1. which day? 2. any day; someday
哪些(?) **nǎ xiē** 1. which of those? 2. any of those
哪怕 **nǎ pà** no matter

丨	口	口	叮	叮	叮	呀	哪
哪	哪	哪	哪			

Hanyu Pinyin Index

Radical Index

1 stroke

[一]

一	yī	10
二	èr	11
七	qī	16
三	sān	12
下	xià	103
五	wǔ	14
不	bù	60
再	zài	53
两	liǎng	85
哥	gē	67
事	shì	84

[丨]

中	zhōng/zhòng	39

[丿]

九	jiǔ	18
生	shēng	38
年	nián	96

[乙]

了	le/liǎo	108
也	yě	59

2 strokes

[卜]

上	shàng	102

[十]

十	shí	19
午	wǔ	104

[冂]

同	tóng	45

八 [丷]

八	bā	17
弟	dì	69

人 [亻]

人	rén	57
个	gè	86
今	jīn	91
什	shén/shí	30
他	tā	27
们	men	50
你	nǐ	20
住	zhù	71
做	zuò	83

[儿]

儿	ér/r	75

[几]

几	jǐ/jī	93

[亠]

六	liù	15

[讠]

谁	shéi/shuí	61
请	qǐng	23
课	kè	42
谢	xiè	52

[阝]

那	nà/nèi	76
都	dōu/dū	80

[厶]

么	me	31

[又]

友	yǒu	49

3 strokes

[土]

在	zài	72

[艹]

英	yīng	40

[小]

小	xiǎo	47
少	shǎo/shào	88

[大]

大	dà	36
天	tiān	92

[口]

叫	jiào	29
号	hào	94
吃	chī	105
吗	ma	58
呢	ne	51
哪	nǎ/něi	109

[囗]

四	sì	13
国	guó	56

[巾]

师	shī	44

[夕]

名	míng	32
多	duō	87

[饣]

饭	fàn	107

[门]

问	wèn	24
间	jiān	90

[氵]

没	méi	81

English–Chinese Index

A

a(n) 一 yī *10*

a(n) (of something) 一个 yī ge *10*

a couple 两口子 liǎng kǒu zi *85*

a guest room 一间客房 yī jiān kè fáng *90*

a little 一点儿 yī diǎnr *75*; 有点儿 yǒu diǎnr *82*

a long time 好久 hǎo jiǔ *22*

a moment 一会儿 yí huìr *75*

a short while 一会儿 yí huìr *75*; 一下 yí xià *103*

about 差不多 chà bu duō *87*

above 上/上面 shàng/shàng mian *102*

address (residence) 住址 zhù zhǐ *71*

adult 大人/成人 dà rén/chéng rén *57*

after a meal 饭后 fàn hòu *107*

afternoon (p.m.) 下午/午后 xià wǔ/wǔ hòu *104*

afternoon nap 午觉/午睡 wǔ jiào/wǔ shuì *104*

afterwards/after the event 事后 shì hòu *84*

again 再 zài *53*

again and again 再三/一再 zài sān/yí zài *53*

age 年纪 nián ji *96*

air stewardess 空姐 kōng jiě *68*

alike 同样 tóng yàng *45*

all 都 dōu *80*

all are 都是 dōu shì *80*

all at once 一下子 yí xià zi *79*

all have 都有 dōu yǒu *80*

all have gone to school 都上学了 dōu shàng xué le *108*

all know how to do 都会 dōu huì *80*

all of a sudden 一下子 yí xià zi *79*

almost 几 jī *93*

almost, nearly 几乎 jī hū *93*

almost complete 七七八八 qī qī bā bā *16*

alright 好 hǎo *22*; 没事 méi shì *81*

alright? 好吗? hǎo ma *58*

alright then ... 那好 nà hǎo *22*

also 也 yě *59*

alumni 校友 xiào yǒu *46*

always 老是 lǎo shì *35*

...and... 和 hé *65*

amazing 了不起 liǎo bu qǐ *108*

amiable 和气 hé qì *65*

among 中 zhōng *39*

ancient 古老 gǔ lǎo *43*

angry 生气 shēng qì *38*

anxious 七上八下 qī shàng bā xià *16*

any 哪/哪个 nǎ/nǎ ge *109*

any of those 哪些 nǎ xiē *109*

any day 哪天 nǎ tiān *109*

anyone 哪个 nǎ ge *109*

anytime 几时 jǐ shí *93*

April 四月 sì yuè *13*

arrogant 自大 zì dà *36*

ask 问 wèn *24*

at 在 zài *72*

at home 在家里 zài jiā lǐ *72*

at night 夜间 yè jiān *90*

at present 今 jīn *91*

at the same time 同时 tóng shí *45*

at the worst 大不了 dà bu liǎo *36*

at what time? 什么时候 shén me shí hòu *30*

attend 上 shàng *102*

attend class 上课 shàng kè *42*

August 八月 bā yuè *17*

aunt (father's married sister) 姑妈 gū mā *66*

aunt (mother's married sister) 姨妈 yí mā *66*

B

be 在 zài *72*

be an upright person 做人 zuò rén *83*

be called 叫/叫做 jiào/jiào zuò *29*

be late 晚点 wǎn diǎn *106*

beautiful 美/美丽 měi/měi lì *55*

beautiful girl 美女 měi nǚ *55*

beautiful woman 美人 měi rén *55*

become famous 出名 chū míng *32*

before a meal 饭前 fàn qián *107*

beforehand 事前 shì qián *84*

belittle 小看 xiǎo kàn *47*

below 下面 xià mian *103*

between 间/中间 jiān/zhōng jiān *39, 90*

don't have 没有 méi yǒu *81*

don't know 不会 bú huì *60*

don't mention it 不谢 búxiè *52*; 不客气 bú kè qi *60*

don't want 不要 bú yào *60*

E

each one 个个/每个 gè gè/měi ge *86*

early 早 zǎo *101*

early date 早日 zǎo rì *101*

early in the morning 一早 yī zǎo *101*

earlier time/early stage 早期 zǎo qī *100*

eat 吃 chī *105*

eat raw food 生吃 shēng chī *38*

eaten/eaten enough 吃饱了 chī bǎo le *105*

eight 八 bā *17*

eight-hundred and five 八百零五 bā bǎi líng wǔ *17*

eighteen 十八 shì bā *17*

eighth 第八 dì bā *17*

80 per cent 八成 bā chéng *17*

eighty-two 八十二 bā shí èr *17*

eldest brother 大哥 dà gē *67*

eldest sibling 老大 lǎo dà *43*

eldest sister 大姐 dà jiě *68*

eldest son 大儿子 dà ér zi *75*

eleven 十一 shí yī *10*

embarassed 不好意思 bù hǎo yì si *60*

England 英国 yīng guó *40*

English language 英语 yīng yǔ *40*

English language (written) 英文 yīng wén *40*

etc 什么的 shén me de *30*

even 都 dōu *80*

even to the point that 什至 shén zhì *30*

evening 晚上 wǎn shang *106*

evening shift 晚班 wǎn bān *106*

every day 天天/每天 tiān tiān/měi tiān *92*; 每日 měi rì *98*

every family 每家/家家 měi jiā/jiā jiā *63*

every matter 事事/每事 shì shì/měi shì *84*

every year 年年/每年 nián nián/měi nián *96*

everybody 大家 dà jiā *36*

everyone 人人/每人 rén rén/měi rén *57*

everyone in a family 一家大小 yī jiā dà xiǎo *63*

everywhere 四处 sì chù *13*

excuse me 不好意思 bù hǎo yì si *60*

expensive 贵 guì *25*

expire 到期 dào qī *100*

express appreciation 答谢 dá xiè *52*

F

fall sick 生病 shēng bìng *38*

fame 名 míng *32*

family 家/家庭 jiā/jiā tíng *63*

family member 家人 jiā rén *63*

famous person 名人 míng rén *32*

fantastic 了不起 liǎo bu qǐ *108*

father 爸/爸爸/老爸 bà/bà ba/lǎo bà *64*

far more 多 duō *87*

February 二月 èr yuè *11*

fellow worker 工友 gōng yǒu *49*

female 女 nǚ *74*

female gender 女性 nǚ xìng *74*

female student 女生 nǚ shēng *74*

few 少 shǎo *88*

fifteen 十五 shí wǔ *14*

fifth 第五 dì wǔ *14*

fifty 五十 wǔ shí *14*

finish (attending) 下 xià *103*

finish (doing) 做好/做完 zuò hǎo/zuò wán *83*

finish class 下课 xià kè *42*

finish school for the day 放学 fàng xué *37*

finish work 下班 xià bān *103*

first 第一 dì yī *10*

first in position 第一名 dì yī míng *32*

first lesson 第一课 dì yī kè *42*

first younger sister 大妹 dà mèi *70*

five 五 wǔ *14*

five (books) 五本 wǔ běn *14*

five years 五年 wǔ nián *14*

follower 徒弟 tú dì *69*

foreign country 外国 wài guó *56*

foreigner 老外 lǎo wài *43*

forget it 算了 suàn le *108*

T

table 桌子 zhuō zi *79*

take leave 请假 qǐng jià *23*

tasty 好吃 hǎo chī *105*

teacher 老师 lǎo shī *43, 44*; 教师 jiào shī *44*

teacher and student 师生 shī shēng *44*

teenage girl 少女 shào nǚ *88*

teenager 青少年 qīng shào nián *88*

temporarily 一时 yī shí *89*

ten 十 shí *19*

ten points 十分 shí fēn *19*

tend to 多少 duō shǎo *87*

tenth 第十 dì shí *19*

tenth (mathematics) 什 shí *30*

tenth (of a month) 十号 shí hào *94*

text 课文 kè wén *42*

textbook 课本 kè běn *42*

thank 谢 xiè *52*

thank you 谢谢 xiè xie *52*

thank you speech 谢词 xiè cí *52*

that 那 nà *76*

that (one) 那个 nà ge *76, 86*

that type 那样 nà yàng *76*

That's right! 对了 duì le *108*

the same 同样 tóng yàng *45*; 没两样 méi liǎng yàng *85*

their (female) 她们的 tā men de *28*

their (male) 他们的 tā men de *27*

theirs (female) 她们的 tā men de *28*

theirs (male) 他们的 tā men de *27*

them (female) 她们 tā men *28*

them (male) 他们 tā men *27*

then 那么 nà me *76*

there 那里/那儿/那边 nà li/nàr/nà biān *76*

there's only... 只有 zhǐ yǒu *82*

these 这些 zhè xiē *73*

they (female) 她们 tā men *28*

they (male) 他们 tā men *27*

third 第三 dì sān *12*

third younger sister 三妹 sān mèi *70*

thirteen 十三 shí sān *12*

thirty 三十 sān shí *12*

this 这 zhè *73*

this evening 今晚 jīn wǎn *91*

this month 这个月 zhè ge yuè *97*

this morning 今早 jīn zǎo *91*

this one 这个 zhè ge *73, 86*

this time 这次 zhè cì *73*

this way 这样 zhè yàng *73*

this year 今年 jīn nián *91*

those 那些 nà xiē *76*

three 三 sān *12*

three months 三个月 sān ge yuè *12*

Thursday 星期四 xīng qī sì *13*

time 时/时间 shí/shí jiān *89, 90*; 日子 rì zi *98*

to be 是 shì *35*

to be or not to be 是不是 shì bu shì *35*

to invite 请 qǐng *23*

today 今天 jīn tiān *91*; 今日 jīnrì *91, 98*

together 一同/一起 yī tóng/yī qǐ *10, 45*

tomorrow 明天 míng tiān *92, 95*; 明日 míng rì *95, 98*

tomorrow morning 明早 míng zǎo *101*

tonight 今晚 jīn wǎn *91*

too 也 yě *59*

too expensive 太贵了 tài guì le *25*

top 上面 shàng mian *102*

topic (of lessons) 课题 kè tí *42*

treat 请客 qǐng kè *23*

trivial matter 小事 xiǎo shì *84*

Tuesday 星期二 xīng qī èr *11*

twelve 十二 shí èr *11*

twenty 二十 èr shí *11*

20 per cent discount 八折 bā zhé *17*

twice 两次 liǎng cì *85*

two 两 liǎng *85*

two (number) 二 èr *11*

two doors 两个门 liǎng ge mén *86*

two hundred 两百 liǎng bǎi *85*

two months 两个月 liǎng ge yuè *85*

two types 两样 liǎng yàng *85*

U

unbearable 受不了 shòu bu liǎo *108*

under 下 xià *103*

underestimate 小看 xiǎo kàn *47*
underneath 下面 xià mian *103*
understand 明白 míng bai *95*
United States of America 美国 měi guó *55*
unlikely 不会 bú huì *60*
up to now 至今 zhì jīn *91*
urine/urinate 小便 xiǎo biàn *47*
us 我们/咱们 wǒ men/zán men *34, 50*

V

valuable 贵/名贵 guì/míng guì *25*
vehicle (small scale) 车子 chē zi *79*
very 十分 shí fēn *19*
very beautiful 很美/太美了 hěn měi/tài měi le *55*
very few/little 很少 hěn shǎo *88*
very good 很好 hěn hǎo *22*
VIP 贵客/贵宾 guì kè/guì bīn *25*
visit 访问 fǎng wèn *24*

W

washroom 洗手间 xǐ shǒu jiān *90*
we 我们/咱们 wǒ men/zán men *34, 50*
weather 天气 tiān qì *92*
Wednesday 星期三 xīng qī sān *12*
week 星期 xīng qī *99*
well-known 出名 chū míng *32*
what 什么 shén me *30, 31*
what's up? 有事吗? yǒu shì ma *58*
what date? 几号? jǐ hào *94*
what kind? 哪样? nǎ yàng *109*
what size? 几号? jǐ hào *94*
what time? 几点? jǐ diǎn *93*
whatever 哪样 nǎ yàng *109*
when? 什么时候? shén me shí hòu *30*; 几时? jǐ shí *93*
when the time comes 到时 dào shí *89*
where? 哪里? nǎ li *109*
Where's the person? 人呢? rén ne *51*
whether or not 有没有? yǒu méi yǒu *82*
which? 哪?/哪个?nǎ/nǎ ge *109*
which day? 哪天? nǎ tiān *109*

which number? 几号? jǐ hào *94*
which of those? 哪些? nǎ xiē *109*
who 谁 shéi/shuí *61*
whose 谁的 shéi de *61, 62*
why? 为什么? wèi shén me *31*
wife 女人 nǚ rén *74*; 妻子 qī zi *79*
wife (informal) 老婆 lǎo po *43*
win a prize 中奖 zhòng jiǎng *39*
wise 英明 yīng míng *40*
without 没 méi *81*
woman 女人 nǚ rén *74*; 妇女 fù nǚ *74*
wonderful 美好 měi hǎo *55*
work 做工 zuò gōng *83*; 做事 zuò shì *84*
worker 工人 gōng rén *57*
worry 七上八下 qī shàng bā xià *16*
write word 写字 xiě zì *33*
written character 字 zì *33*
written language 文 wén *41*
writing 文/文字 wén/wén zì *41*

Y

yeah 是啊 shì a *35*
year 年 nián *96*
year after next year 后年 hòu nián *96*
year before last year 前年 qián nián *96*
yell 叫喊 jiào hǎn *29*
yes 是/是的/是啊 shì/shì de/shì a *35*
yesterday 昨天 zuó tiān *92*; 昨日 zuó rì *98*
you 你 nǐ *20*
you (plural) 你们 nǐ men *20, 50*
you (polite) 您 nín *21*
young 少 shào *88*
younger brother 弟/弟弟 dì/dì di *69*
younger brother and sister 弟妹 dì mèi *69*
younger brother's wife 弟妹 dì mèi *69*
younger sister 妹/妹妹 mèi/mèi mei *70*
youngest sister 小妹 xiǎo mèi *70*
youngest son 小儿子 xiǎo ér zi *75*
your family name? 您贵姓? nín guì xìng *21*
your honorable surname? 贵姓 guì xìng *25*
your/yours 你的 nǐ de *20, 62*
your/yours (plural) 你们的 nǐ men de *20*

List of Radicals

— 1 stroke —

1 丶 dot
2 一 one
3 丨 down
4 丿 left
5 ㇟ "back-turned stroke"
6 ㇆ "top of 刁"
7 乙 twist

— 2 strokes —

8 冫 ice
9 亠 lid
10 讠 (side-) words
11 二 two
12 十 ten
13 厂 slope
14 ナ "top of 左"
15 匚 basket
16 卜 (上) divine
17 刂 (side) knife
18 冖 crown
19 冂 borders
20 𠂉 "top of 每"
21 亻 (side-)man
22 厃 "top of 后"
23 人 (入) person (enter)
24 八 (丷) eight
25 乂 "bottom of 义"
26 勹 wrap
27 刀 (夕) knife
28 力 strength
29 儿 son
30 几 (几) table
31 ㄅ "top of 予"
32 卩 seal
33 阝 (on the left) mound
34 阝 (on the right) city
35 又 right hand
36 乏 march
37 厶 cocoon
38 凵 bowl
39 匕 ladle

— 3 strokes —

40 氵 "three-dots water"
41 忄 (side-) heart
42 爿 bed
43 亡 to flee
44 广 lean-to
45 宀 roof
46 门 gate
47 辶 halt
48 工 work
49 土 (士) earth (knight)
50 艹 grass
51 廾 clasp
52 大 big
53 尢 lame
54 寸 thumb
55 扌 (side-) hand
56 弋 dart
57 巾 cloth

58 口 mouth
59 囗 surround
60 山 mountain
61 巾 sprout
62 彳 step
63 彡 streaks
64 夕 dusk
65 夊 follow, slow
66 丸 bullet
67 尸 corpse
68 飠 (side-) food
69 犭 (side-) dog
70 彐 (ヨ,且) pig's head
71 弓 bow
72 己 (巳) self
73 女 woman
74 子 (孑) child
75 马 horse
76 幺 coil
77 纟 (糸) silk
78 巛 river
79 小 (⺍) small

— 4 strokes —

80 灬 "fire-dots"
81 心 heart
82 斗 peck
83 火 fire
84 文 pattern
85 方 square
86 户 door
87 礻 (side-) sign
88 王 king
89 龶 "top of 青"
90 天 (夭) heaven (tender)
91 韦 walk off
92 少 "top of 老"
93 廿 twenty
94 木 tree
95 不 not
96 犬 dog
97 歹 chip
98 瓦 tile
99 牙 tooth
100 车 car
101 戈 lance
102 止 toe
103 日 sun
104 曰 say
105 中 middle
106 贝 cowrie
107 见 see
108 父 father
109 气 breath
110 牛 cow
111 手 hand
112 毛 fur
113 攵 knock
114 片 slice
115 斤 ax
116 爪 (爫) claws
117 尺 foot (length)
118 月 moon/meat

119 殳 club
120 欠 yawn
121 风 wind
122 氏 clan
123 比 compare
124 聿 "top of 书"
125 水 water

— 5 strokes —

126 立 stand
127 疒 sick
128 穴 cave
129 衤 (side-) gown
130 夫 "top of 春"
131 玉 jade
132 示 sign
133 去 go
134 龹 "top of 劳"
135 甘 sweet
136 石 rock
137 龙 dragon
138 戊 halberd
139 ⺌ "top of 常"
140 业 business
141 目 eye
142 田 field
143 由 from
144 申 stretch
145 罒 net
146 皿 dish
147 钅 (side-) gold
148 矢 arrow
149 禾 grain
150 白 white
151 瓜 melon
152 鸟 bird
153 皮 skin
154 癶 back
155 矛 spear
156 疋 bolt

— 6 strokes —

157 羊 (䒑, 㸸) sheep
158 关 roll
159 米 rice
160 齐 line-up
161 衣 gown
162 亦 (亦) also
163 耳 ear
164 臣 bureaucrat
165 龷 "top of 栽"
166 西 (覀) cover (west)
167 東 thorn
168 亚 inferior
169 而 beard
170 页 head
171 至 reach
172 光 light
173 虍 tiger
174 虫 bug
175 缶 crock
176 耒 plow
177 舌 tongue

178 竹 (⺮) bamboo
179 臼 mortar
180 自 small nose
181 血 blood
182 舟 boat
183 羽 wings
184 艮 (㠯) stubborn

— 7 strokes —

185 言 words
186 辛 bitter
187 辰 early
188 麦 wheat
189 走 walk
190 赤 red
191 豆 flask
192 束 bundle
193 酉 wine
194 豕 pig
195 里 village
196 足 foot
197 采 cull
198 豸 snake
199 谷 valley
200 身 torso
201 角 horn

— 8 strokes —

202 青 green
203 卓 "side of 朝"
204 雨 rain
205 非 wrong
206 齿 teeth
207 黾 toad
208 隹 dove
209 金 gold
210 鱼 fish

— 9 strokes —

211 音 tone
212 革 hide
213 是 be
214 骨 bone
215 香 scent
216 鬼 ghost
217 食 food

— 10 strokes —

218 高 tall
219 鬲 cauldron
220 髟 hair

— 11 strokes —

221 麻 hemp
222 鹿 deer

— 12 strokes —

223 黑 black

— 13 strokes —

224 鼓 drum
225 鼠 mouse
226 鼻 big nose